Rollins College
Book-A-Year

Gift of
William Hartmeyer
in honor of
Emily Hartmeyer

The Legend of Lasseter's Reef

Mark Greenwood

Readers who might be distressed by seeing photographs of people who have died should take care when reading this book.

CYGNET BOOKS

Silhouetted against the fiery glow of sunset, a wanderer dragged his weary bones across the scorching plains of Central Australia. The search for gold had driven him many miles from water. His clothes were ragged and torn, his tongue swollen from thirst.

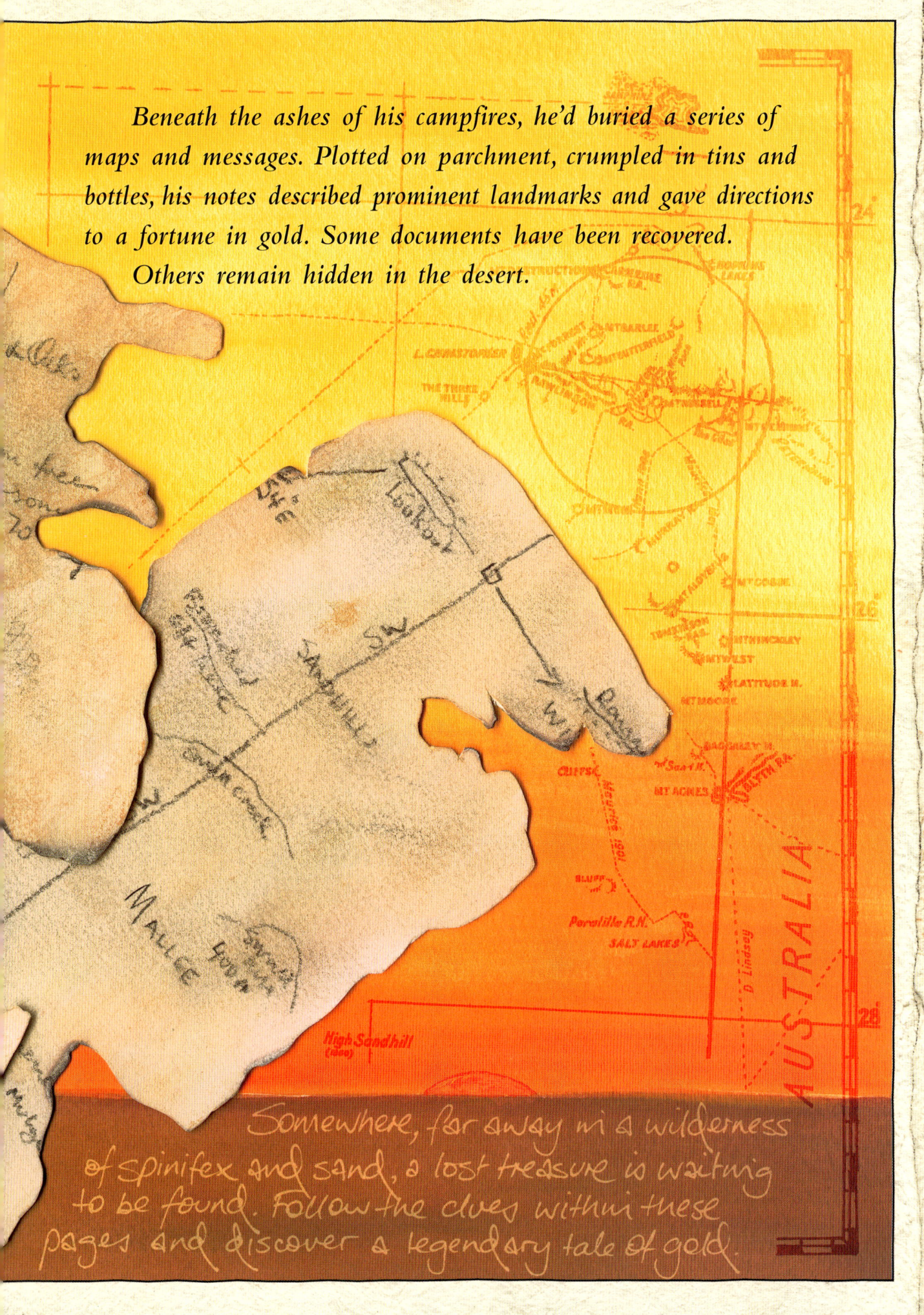

Beneath the ashes of his campfires, he'd buried a series of maps and messages. Plotted on parchment, crumpled in tins and bottles, his notes described prominent landmarks and gave directions to a fortune in gold. Some documents have been recovered. Others remain hidden in the desert.

Somewhere, far away in a wilderness of spinifex and sand, a lost treasure is waiting to be found. Follow the clues within these pages and discover a legendary tale of gold.

1897 During the late 1800s, rumours spread of a cave of gold and a mountain of blood-red rubies hidden in ancient canyons. Wary explorers, haunted by the terrors of thirst and starvation, warned of parched and perilous inland trails littered with sunbleached bones.

ALADDIN'S CAVE OF GOLD
IN HISTORY AND LEGEND

PERILOUS RIDE IN PARCHING DESERT

Gold-Seekers Race Against Death From Thirst

LIVES SHOULD NOT BE RISKED
On Vain Searches In Desert

The facts, rumors, and fancies of the past 36 years, since that first excitement about the rich gold which Earle reported, or was credited with reporting, in the Tomkinson Ranges, have become so confused, that, out of the few bald facts, there has grown up a romantic story worthy of the pages of a fairy tale. In an endeavor to arrive at the true facts of the case, old hands, including J. Lamb, W. R. Murray, Alec Ross, and L. A. Wells, have been sought out, and, from the memories of the past, stage by stage, the story of Earle's find has been pieced together, till at length one may, with a measure of confidence, tell it true to fact. No one account of the incident tallies with another, we hoped, of all Ranges. The result was that a syndicate was formed to examine the discovery in greater detail.

Story Of Tragedy

At this period Earle, suffering with cancer of the eye, was unable to enter the bush, and it was not till 1900 that Albert, with Cockrum, Cockrum junior, one of the Worman brothers, and Undler, an Afghan camel-driver, set out from Oodnadatta for the far away ranges. They were supplied by Earle with a plan indicating a place two and a half miles north of Mount Davis, but whether it was meant to indicate the site of the cave or a likely place to try for gold is not quite clear. The trip lasted from October, 1900, till January, 1901.

Undaunted by the dangers of uncharted land, a 17-year-old adventurer, Harold Lasseter, set out on a quest to seek his fortune. Starting from Queensland, he crossed the country on horseback. Mile after mile he rode, over rugged mountain ranges rising from the arid plains. Days turned to weeks, weeks to months.

MAP OF
AUSTRALIA
SHOWING THE
UNEXPLORED PORTIONS

I followed the lay of the country from hill to hill, with deviations over the plains, but found the hilly country best for water and game.

Lasseter arrived at the ruby fields only to find the gems were garnets—practically worthless. Determined to find his fortune, he worked his way west on a slow ride through the wilderness. Mirages of water shimmered on the horizon as he veered southwards to avoid a vast sea of sand. On and on he rode, swaying to and fro, in sweltering heat.

He followed the bellbird's song to a tiny oasis of water. While resting his horse, he noticed several piles of unusual stones that flickered and flashed in the sunlight. Lasseter pushed back his hat and inspected them. They were heavy in his hands, and peppered with fine yellow flakes. His heart pounded. A smile spread over his sunburnt face. Some of the stones were criss-crossed with thin veins of pure gold.

Following a crumbling reef of gold as it dipped into the red earth, then reappeared, Lasseter filled an oatmeal bag with specimens. With trembling hands, he sketched a map, noting the position of nearby mountain peaks. "The reef is worth a fortune," he thought. "It's the find of a lifetime!"

With his exhausted horse unable to continue, Lasseter set off on foot to register a claim, but with each step the country became more hostile. Thirsty desert oaks withered on the plains. His skin burned and blistered as he trudged on, clutching his heavy bag.

After four days without water, weak and delirious from the heat, Lasseter dropped to the ground. He crawled until his knees were blood-raw. A murder of crows circled overhead, waiting patiently for Lasseter to draw his last breath.

The reef is near a salt lake and three hills that look like three women in sunbonnets. 35 miles to the south-east is another hill like a Quaker hat — tall, conical in shape, with its top cut off.

By chance, an Afghan cameleer was slowly wending his way across the desert, collecting sandalwood. As he rode closer he could make out Lasseter's ragged form, barely alive. The Afghan held his canteen to the dying man's parched lips, helped him onto his camel and led him along a stock trail to a surveyor's camp.

Afghan cameleer Faizal Deen, c. 1898. The exact identity of Lasseter's rescuer is unknown.

To find the reef again I would prefer to go in from the NW Stock Route, about the 23rd Parallel. There may be a better way from Laverton.

Under the watchful eye of Surveyor Harding, Lasseter was nursed back to life with food and precious water. While Lasseter rested, Harding examined the contents of the bag. The specimens were magnificent! The rich glint of gold was visible in every stone. Harding begged Lasseter to take him to the reef, but after his recent brush with death the young adventurer was in no hurry to return.

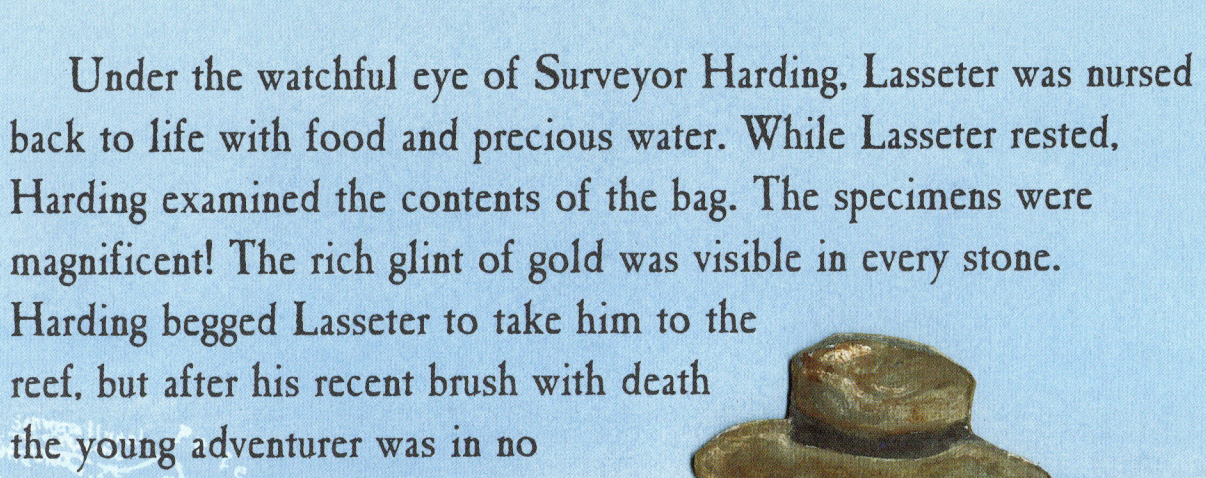

Three years later, guided by landmarks, Lasseter relocated the reef with Harding. They took compass bearings, but on return their watches were found to be faulty. The time error meant their recording of the exact location of the reef was out by hundreds of miles. Lasseter tried in vain to equip another expedition, but a dangerous journey into the unknown did not appeal to wary investors.

1930 Lasseter's remarkable discovery remained a closely guarded secret until 1930, when Australia was in the grip of the Great Depression. Like many, Lasseter found himself out of work, unable to support his young family. In troubled times, when people were searching for hope, his story interested a group of mining men.

Lewis Harold Bell Lasseter

"Gentlemen," Lasseter began, "I have a proposition for you. For the past thirty-three years I have known of a vast gold-bearing reef…" The men drew their chairs closer and questioned Lasseter thoroughly. The room buzzed with excitement. When satisfied that he could guide them to a fortune, the eager investors formed the Central Australian Gold Exploration Company. An agreement was drawn up for Lasseter to lodge a sealed envelope containing directions to his amazing discovery with a Sydney bank, for safekeeping.

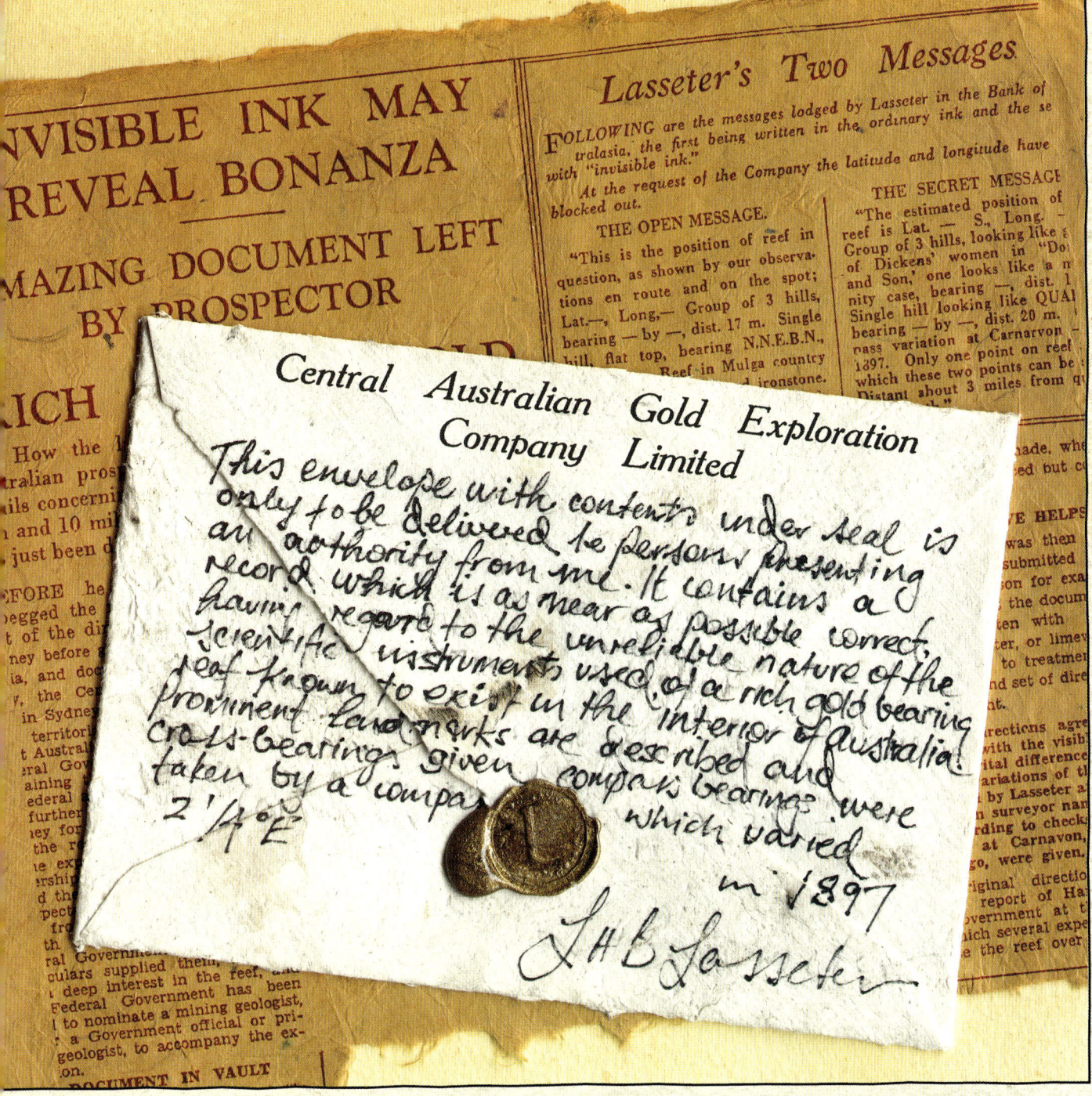

With Lasseter as guide, a team of specially chosen men set out in a truck from Alice Springs. An aeroplane, the *Golden Quest*, followed to relay supplies to their campsites. The truck blazed trails through soft sand, and cleared thickets of mulga to form makeshift runways. Across broad plateaus they drove, through wind and choking dust.

Expedition truck

At the close of day, as moonlight bathed the desert, the men pitched camp, repaired punctures and boiled the billy. At Ilbilla they shared the underground springwaters with a dingo trapper and his team of camels. As they ate damper and took bearings by the stars, Lasseter picked up a stick and drew a sand map. "The three hills look like three sisters," he whispered as the campfire crackled. "Nearby there's a salt lake and a tall, flat-topped hill."

Expedition team (Lasseter in front)

The reef is in mulga cantry and is quartz and ironstone. The quartz has the reddish tinge of the surrounding country. It is possible for a plane to land near the reef. It can be seen just peeping through the mulga.

But, after weeks of searching, disaster struck the expedition. The wing of the *Golden Quest* clipped a tree as the plane took off. It struck the ground, bored into the sand and flipped over. Petrol dripped onto sizzling metal as the injured pilot struggled to escape from the twisted wreckage.

Wreckage of the Golden Quest

A few days later, the truck was engulfed in flames when dry grass and twigs ignited beneath the overheated engine. Beaten by the brutal heat, with no gold in sight, the men began to whisper their doubts about continuing. Finally, when Lasseter climbed to the top of a high mountain look-out and announced, "We're 150 miles too far north," the exhausted men decided to abandon the expedition.

Worried that other fortune hunters might beat him to the gold, Lasseter hastily made arrangements to hire the trapper's team of camels to continue the search. "A thousand miles of desert won't stop me," he told the others. "If I don't find gold, I'm never coming back."

Last photograph of Lasseter

Proceed to Sandstone Rock Reservoir, through the Rawlinson Range to Lake Christopher. Look for a message in the centre one of three fires on the lake.

The camels swayed from side to side in steady rhythm as Lasseter zigzagged through the mountain ranges, searching the horizon for his landmarks. Crossing Lake Amadeus, they sank to their knees as the soft salt crust split and cracked. They bellowed and roared as Lasseter struggled to free them from the slimy ooze.

Lasseter trekked through the gap in Bowley's Range, between the Shaw and Irvine rivers, across Livingstone Pass. He prospected a creek near Gordon Springs and marked a lone tree with instructions. Beneath the ruby embers of his campfire, he buried a tin containing secret letters and maps.

I had to go right out to Lake Christopher, which is 100 miles across the WA border, to get my bearings. Then I went directly to the reef.

After many weary weeks in the saddle, Lasseter finally recognised his country. The "three sisters" could not be mistaken. To the southeast was the other flat-topped hill. The gold he had searched for was now within his grasp.

Just as he had many years ago, Lasseter followed the crumbling outcrop, mesmerised by the precious yellow sparkle in the stone. Once again a staggering fortune in gold stood before him.

Anxious to head back and inform the others of his success, Lasseter took samples and pegged the locality of the reef, marking out the boundaries with posts to stake his claim.

I've pegged the reef. The datum post is sticking in a waterhole on a quartz blow. I made the run in 5 days.

Spirals of dust rose from the camel tracks as Lasseter retraced his journey. Thirsty from the long ride, he stopped to boil a billy with his last drops of water. An emu darted about in nearby scrub, its feathers puffed up to protect its young. The frightened camels bucked and reared, kicking their way free from a tangle of ropes. Lopsided supply loads crashed to the ground. Lasseter collected a blanket, some rice, tins of beef and other supplies that had shaken free, as his camels thundered out of sight.

Lasseter stumbled on through thickets of mulga. He followed the winding course of a dry river, and took shelter in a cave. By day, tormented by flies and swarms of bull ants, Lasseter thought of his wife and children and waited for rescue. At night, as a cold wind whistled through the valley, he wrote in a diary and dreamed of gold.

Smoke from his campfires attracted a nomadic family of Pitjantjatjara and Pintupi people. An elder befriended him, offering him rabbit, berries and ground-up seeds to eat, but Lasseter could only manage meagre mouthfuls.

As days turned to weeks, Lasseter endured the agony of slow starvation. He became weaker and weaker, a living skeleton, helpless as a kitten. Every day he searched the sky for a plane, hoping for relief. Every day he was disappointed.

Pipanytji, the Aboriginal elder who befriended Lasseter

His one slim chance of survival was to try an 80-mile trek to the distant domes of the Olgas. "Perhaps a rescue party will reach me there," he thought, "near shade and cool, fresh water."

Before leaving the cave, he hid maps and notes beneath the coals of his campfires. On a tree outside the cave, Lasseter carved a message to indicate where he had buried his diary.

Marked tree outside Lasseter's cave

I'm an awful sight. The skeleton of me can scarcely support the weight of my clothes. The flies and ants have nearly eaten my face away.

Beneath the blazing sun Lasseter limped painfully through clumps of prickly spinifex until, sick and weak, his eyes blinded by dust, he could walk no further. The elder, who had followed his trail, fashioned a stretcher from branches and dragged him to shade. Here, sheltered from the sun's fierce rays, he made Lasseter comfortable on a bed of bark and gently pillowed his head.

Alice Springs locals said that summer was "so hot that even the snakes stayed home". Bushman Bob Buck, a renowned tracker, was hired by the company to find Lasseter.

Bushman Bob Buck

Looking along the line of the reef in a north-westerly direction the "three sisters" seem to be sitting on the far end of the reef.

Buck searched a thousand miles in eleven weeks. He followed tracks to the ridge where the camels had bolted and uncovered tins containing partly burned maps and messages. At the top end of a cave, beneath a rock ledge, he dug up Lasseter's cloth-covered diary.

While Buck was camped at a soak north of the Petermann Ranges, Pitjantjatjara men approached his camp and beckoned him to follow. By the banks of a dry creek, he found a low mound of earth, a lonely grave, covered by a canopy of bush.

Bob Buck questions Pitjantjatjara men

Marked tree in Lasseter country

Drifting sands have swept away Lasseter's tracks but many still search for his gold. Adventurers have studied the vague and mysterious directions he lodged with the bank. Lasseter's diary and maps wrapped in the wrinkled leather of his kitbag have been carefully examined. But all who seek his treasure have failed. Perhaps other clues remain hidden in rusted tins, buried beneath the ashes of his old campfires.

When the moon is full and the dingoes howl, some say a restless spirit wanders the ancient plains of Central Australia. Legend has it that somewhere, far away in a wilderness of spinifex and sand, Lasseter's Reef is still waiting to be found.

the reef is a bonanza!

For Frané

Special Thanks
Bob Lasseter, Kylie Powell, Amanda Curtin, Janine Drakeford, David Fosdick, Lesley and Bob Reece, David, Lindsay and Stephanie Lloyd, David and Neil "Nugget" Gibson; all at UWA Press; Children's Book Council of Australia (WA Branch); the Central Land Council—Brian Connelly and Tony Keyes; library staff at Battye Library, State Library of Western Australia, State Records Office of Western Australia, Mitchell Library Collection, State Library of New South Wales, National Archives of Australia, National Library of Australia and Northern Territory Library and Information Service.

Author supported by ArtsWA in association with the Lotteries Commission.

Sources
Bailey, J., "History of Lasseter's Reef", State Library of New South Wales.

Blatchford, T., letter to Central Australian Gold Exploration Co. Ltd (CAGE) Chairman, 18 February 1932, Battye Library.

CAGE Papers, State Library of New South Wales.

Coote, E., *Hell's Airport*, Peterman Press, Sydney, 1934.

Lasseter, H., letter to Minister for Home and Territories, 3 February 1930, National Archives of Australia; letter to Undersecretary of Mines, Perth, 14 February 1930, courtesy Battye Library and Department of Minerals and Energy.

Lasseter's Diary, facsimile copy, Angus & Robertson, Sydney, 1986, extracts by permission of the State Library of New South Wales.

Sydney Guardian, 26 April 1931, article about Lasseter's documents lodged with bank.

Terry, Michael, *Untold Miles*, Selwyn & Blount, London, 1933; *Sand and Sun*, M. Joseph Ltd, London, 1937; *Does Lasseter's Reef Really Exist?*, Thomson Publishing, 1970.

Artwork
"Camels Bolting" art inspired by a painting by A. Holloway in Idriess, I., *Lasseter's Last Ride*, Angus & Robertson, North Ryde, 1980. "Lasseter's Rescue" and "Desert Wanderer" inspired by art by Wolfgang Graesse in Clune, F., *The Incredible Outback Adventure of Burke and Wills*, Angus & Robertson, Sydney, 1971.

Photographs
Courtesy of: CAGE Expedition, 1930, State Library of New South Wales; John Bailey collection, State Library of New South Wales; Michael Terry collection, National Library of Australia; R. Lasseter, personal collection; Northern Territory Library; Battye Library.

First published in 2003 by
University of Western Australia Press
Crawley, Western Australia 6009
www.uwapress.uwa.edu.au
under the Cygnet Books imprint

This book is copyright. Apart from any fair dealing for the purpose of private study, research, criticism or review, as permitted under the Copyright Act 1968, no part may be reproduced by any process without written permission. Enquiries should be made to the publisher.

Copyright © Mark Greenwood 2003

National Library of Australia
Cataloguing-in-Publication entry:

Greenwood, Mark
    The legend of Lasseter's reef.

    For children.
    ISBN 1 876268 99 9.

    I. Title.
    A823.3

Produced by Benchmark Publications, Melbourne
Consultant editor Amanda Curtin
Designed by Mark Greenwood and Sandra Nobes
PrePress by Hell Colour Australia
Printed by BPA Print Group

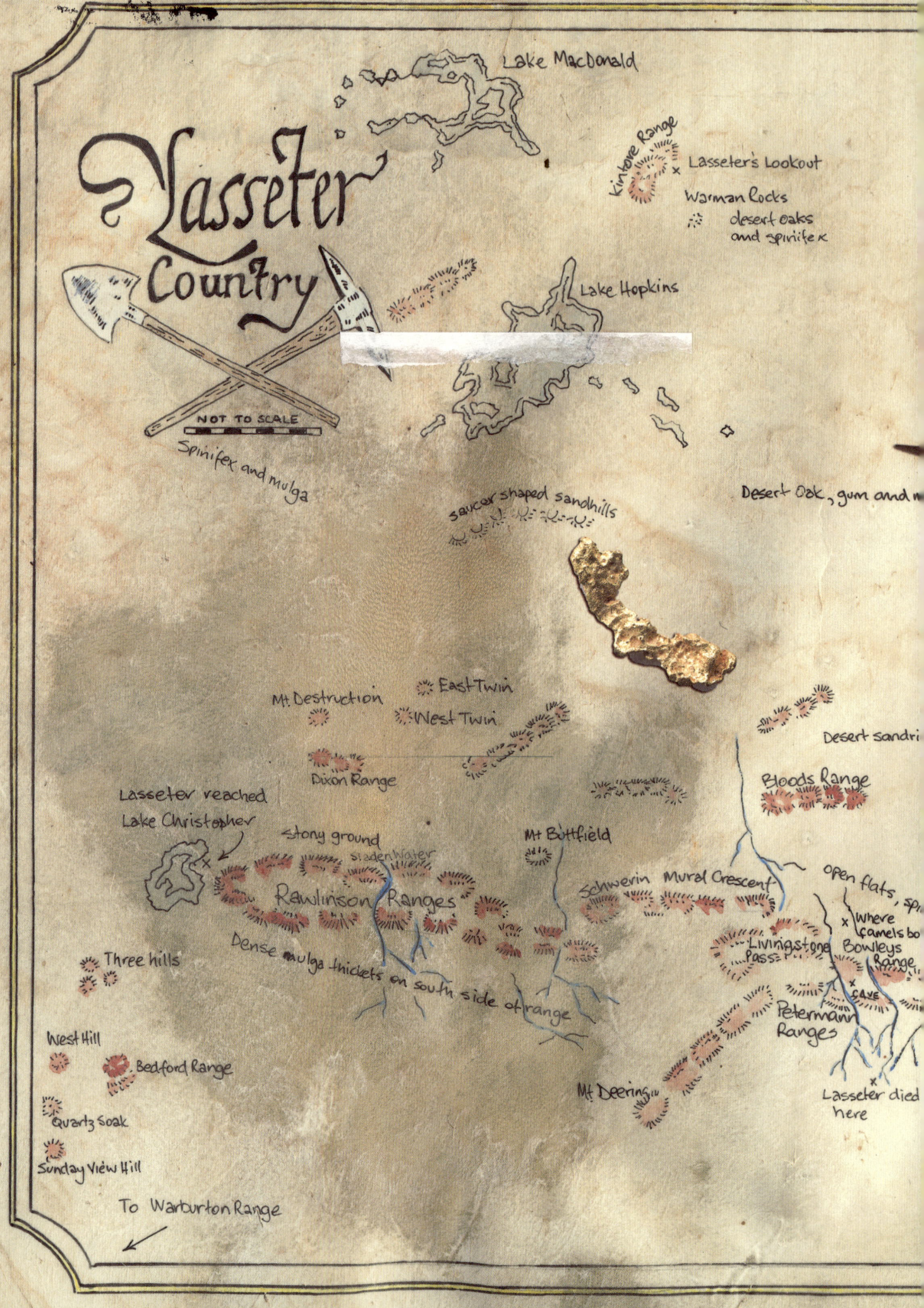